Early in the Mourning

EARLY
IN THE
MOURNING

Daph Willett

GSP

Early in the Mourning
Daph Willett

Published by Greyhound Self-Publishing 2017
Malvern, Worcestershire, United Kingdom.

Designed, printed and bound by Aspect Design
89 Newtown Road, Malvern, Worcs. WR14 1PD
United Kingdom
Tel: 01684 561567
E-mail: allan@aspect-design.net
Website: www.aspect-design.net

Artwork by Roy Willett, Daph Willett and Kelvin Willsher

Cover Design Copyright © 2017 Aspect Design

ISBN 978-1-909219-49-6

To the memory of the loss of our loved ones: Roy, John and Derren. All strength to Kelvin who walks this journey with me now day by day.

Thanks to Nina Shields for her clarity.

To Beth Allen for her counselling, empowerment and support.

Special thanks to Dave and Beryl Eserin for their solidarity of emotional and practical support throughout.

To Ian and Amanda at Iris Print for their patient understanding, which made this book possible. Thank you.

Early in the Mourning

I ask nothing of you
but that you be you.
In this, you will give me much.
You will give me the freedom I need,
Just to be myself.

(1990)

We stand in the shadows of life
'we have no choice'.

Maybe, one day again,
we'll stand in the sun
and rejoice.

(1990)

For John and Derren's loss

Loss and Grief

Please, allow me to grieve in my 'own' way.
I cannot necessarily comply with how you think
I should be grieving.
Let me express my feelings and my needs
if I can, as for me they are real, so please
don't ignore them. I'm in it, this is loss.
Some days, I may not know what I want.
Some days, I may not be able to face anyone
and I need to be alone.
I need time to contemplate, and be miserable and sad.
Some days, I may need to be surrounded by
caring people and seem to be perfectly composed.
Some days, I may lose control.
Be patient, I cannot plan any of this.
It just happens – it's called grief.

(1993)

For Roy

Though you do not
see me weep
My heart it cries it's
silent tears.
How could it not the
deepness feel.
For you were with me
tens of years.

(2016)

Time Now for Loss

This is where I need to stand,
there is no other way.
Somewhere, in the shadows of my grief
I glimpse ahead – a lighter day.
Somewhere ahead, I'll feel the sun
and know it's warmth will then expand.
But now – for this present moment,
this, is where I need to stand.

(2016)

I Don't Like This

So this is loss – I don't like it,
I don't want this – can't you see.
Someone take this grief away,
as feeling angry – feeling sad,
this really isn't me.
How long will this go on for?
Is there a measured time?
Will it be done before too long?
Will I soon be fine?
I want to hurry up this process
and for this hurt to cease
it's aching deep inside me,
and I want to feel some peace.
They say – I have to feel it,
To get through it, then in time
I'll hold you close inside me,
and I'll hold you for all time.
Then I will find some peace in that,
knowing you were mine.
That must be for my future,
when I climb out of this pit,
it doesn't feel like that right now.
This loss just feels, so shit!

(2017)

Unfair

Loss – it eats into your soul
and tears and shreds your day,
when hours seem long, the journey's hard,
It just will not go away.

It's there again tomorrow
through yet another day,
could someone reach inside my heart,
and take this grief away?

I see your image in my dreams
and wake, and you're not there,
we had so much, more life to live
It really isn't fair.

(2016)

Fallen Tears

Never regret your fallen tears
each one a drop of sorrow.
And I shall shed each one for you,
there will be more tomorrow.

They are a measure of your love
and the longing I am feeling.
I'm realizing, just what I've lost
and my senses are still reeling.

At this present moment
all I have is tears,
to show you how I miss you
and will do, through the years.

Tears express the depth of loss,
there is no shame in weeping,
they relieve your mind and soul
and keep your heart from breaking.

(2016)

No Shame

There is no shame in grieving,
To open up and cry.
So feel the loss you're facing,
and beg the question – why?

We are so unaccustomed
in our culture – to be real.
We are encouraged – 'not to cry'
as it's uncomfortable 'to feel'.

So where do you put the feelings,
that brim your very soul.
Where do you put the anger,
that's loosening your control.

This is so natural – this is real,
as love and longing know.
It is something – every one of us
need to face and show.

You don't have to scream or shout,
but if it helps – you can.
Don't turn away from feeling it,
'You're in it' – let it span.

You don't have to weep all night,
though that might be your way.
The ones you lost – acknowledge now,
you'll miss them day by day.

Instant Loss

Instant – like switching off a light.
Can a life so quickly go? –
I stand now helpless in this plight.
My brain now rigid, in it's numbness,
alone and frozen, in the fright.

That tiny, tick of time, that took you from me,
that flick, of second hand, on dial,
It stopped my world forever in this life span,
there is no pretense – and no denial.

A split second, changed my life forever,
through this numbness, I feel fear,
from which right now – I cannot sever,
I am alone, it is very clear.

(1988)

Instant Death

This way is hard
This grief is pain
And I so want you
Back again.

How could you go?
I wasn't ready
Our life was good
And it was steady.

There was no warning
when it came
Then – you were gone
and oh such pain.

Now the emptiness is vast
No time for loves goodbyes
No kisses – holding – fond farewells
All this – is just the past.

(1988)

'The Moment of Loss' Roy 23/3/16

Here I stand, in humble contemplation,
of a life that slipped away today.
I don't yet understand how much my loss means,
I only know I longed for you to stay.

I looked across this shadow darkened room,
your face, as in restful slumber there.
I am comforted, now you look serene
that no longer any pain you have to bear.

I'm riveted in time, just for this moment.
I know so well, what tomorrow brings.
Demands and words and legal actions
and rules and musts, the hymn sheet I must sing.

But in this frozen little time lapse,
I need to be here, and stand with you.
To remember loving moments in my soul place,
that are ours, and no one ever knew.

Now I must sadly, come to leave you.
Farewell – the vision that we shared,
then on this journey I'm now facing,
be within me, knowing that I cared.

In time – I know that this will happen,
In time – as our memories live on,
In time – I'll be glad I held this moment,
Knowing you're at peace, now that you're gone.

(2016)

The Mask

Because I wear a coping mask,
you cannot see me cry.
It is not easy, it is not done,
but each day I try,
to be the way I have to be
to brave it, to get by.

But coping is just the surface,
as deep inside there's pain.
The hollow empty feeling
as I want you back again.
There is an expectation
as the days go by,
that life will get much easier
and I shall not need to cry.

Then I'll begin to smile again
with meaning – not a mask.
As the days will seem much lighter,
life won't be, 'Just a task'.
But for the moment until that time,
I'm where I have to be,
to feel, and hurt, and cry for you,
you were my life, you see.
We were together many years
so I cannot yet be free.

(2016)

Time Warp

The warp of time is transfixed,
in the day, you left my side.
I stand alone in that great loss
on our ever swaying tide.
I ebb and flow, this way and that,
can't see which way to follow,
time hangs upon me like a shroud
and all my depths are hollow.

Oh give my 'now', a reason,
instead of just a then,
when I had a different journey
of what we did and when.
This is the winter of my soul
frozen in this time.
Wisps of grief, like shrouding mist
encompass soul and mind.

Somewhere – in distant future years,
in this journey, as it winds,
hopefully a peace, will grow and stay
and life will seem more kind.
But in this present time warp
the stain of loss, is here,
I must traverse it patiently
before the skies can clear.

(2017)

Realisation

Oh touch my arm, like you used to,
smile your knowing smile.
Hold my hand, with gentleness,
stay with me, for a while.

Then as my vision slowly fades,
reality dawns so clear.
I so long just to feel your touch,
now sadly, you're not here.

Accolade

Let me see your face again
I want to see you smile.
I long to spend some time with you
but for a little while.
It's lonely here without you,
my love I can't defer,
I only want to tell you
how beautiful you were.

(2016)

My Mask

I have a mask I wear each day,
It's hanging by my door.
It's not the one I want to wear
but that can be no more.

So now I wear this new one,
each moment when I'm out.
I smile and talk just like it's me,
but my life's turned inside out.

My act is good, and people think,
that I am healed, and free.
They don't perceive my silent
tears,
or hear my silent plea.

They cannot feel my longing
that nightly haunts my dreams.
How can they comprehend it?
or know what grieving means.

Only if they walk this path,
and wear their masks like me.
So dip their soul in shades of loss,
only then, they'll see.

(2016)

It Isn't Easy

The scars of deepest longing
leave no mark, that you can see.
They hurt and ache inside you,
this is grief, it's what will be.

But I'm impatient on this journey
I stand with mask in place.
And wonder, for how many years,
will this fill my inner space.

I'm told, it isn't easy,
I'm told, it may be slow,
I'm told, grief is unpredictable,
'You must go with the flow'.

The sorrow and the longing,
that now lives in my heart,
will slowly be more bearable,
if I let the healing start.

Comfort

Through this grief – how shall I go?
It is a road I cannot know.
The journey forward seems so slow,
'But fast my heart is beating'.

As each day, the changes made,
cannot make the memories fade.
But for a while to rest they're laid,
'And fast my heart is beating'.

It feels a long and lonely way,
it cannot be hurried, so they say.
Can no one take this grief away?
'So fast my heart is beating'.

Perhaps in time, when enough I've cried,
I'll hold your memory with great pride,
and I'll always live, with you, inside.
'For you, my heart is beating'.

The Carer

Broken – that is how it feels.
Broken – in this space in time.
This loss has shattered life apart,
to want you back – seems like a crime.

Just now, I was a 'carer,'
like all those years – 'forgot'!
Like then, and in that time gone by,
Now – suddenly – I'm not.

For then, there was a purpose,
to care, and love, and try.
So of course your loss, is vast to me.
For you – 'I need to cry'.

And to cry a little for myself,
whose journey is uneven.
Whose status died, in one fell swoop,
and cared, 'twenty-four-seven'.

(2017)

Empty

Oh give my 'Now,' a reason.
Help me readjust.
This crippling hurt, bereavement brings,
to change it is a must.
I know I'm on it's journey,
I know, it will take time.
I've got to find a reason now,
for a life that's only mine.
I am so used to 'Caring',
over ten progressive years.
That not to have that structure,
fills my soul with fears.
Alzheimers, was your master,
with no remorse or care.
It ate your very essence,
until you were not there.
You couldn't feel the love I gave,
your days, seemed far away.
Then as your body failed as well,
sorrow came to stay.
One early rainy, morning,
your spirit slipped away.
With me beside you 'caring',
like every other day.
I'm pleased for you it's over.
What now, will be my lot?
But I'm glad I was your carer then,
as suddenly. I'm not!!

(2016)

'Losing Him, My Child'

When you lose a precious child,
It matters not your creed.
Nor the colour of your skin,
for if we're hurt, we bleed.
The aching heart, a mothers love,
the longing, and the anger.
Why is it, my child had to go?
And now, he's here no longer.

He is so loved, and ever was,
a character in forming.
A valued life, a valued soul,
with sentiment so warming.
There are no words to quantify,
the depth of hollow feeling,
for those of us who share this pain,
whose senses, still are reeling.

Oh parents in this world unite
with tears, that are still falling.
Reach out, with love from in your hearts,
to everyone who's calling.

(2016)

You

You –were just my lovely child.
Loaned a while to me.
To teach me how to love and care,
to contemplate a life to share,
and watch you grow and be.

But oh too soon, the time ran out,
and from my love and care,
you were taken back again,
while I, your mum, must here remain,
in longing, and despair.

And I shall miss you, for all time,
as my life struggles here.
The long long days turn into years,
I'll always weep my silent tears,
as love will ever – always be,
with you, my precious child – you see.

(1990)

Derren –

You are my child,
I wave goodbye,
'Don't be late,'
'No, Mum – I'll try.
That moment –
was the last in time,
that I could hold your hand in mine.

Later –
when your time was come,
too early in your life.
I am so proud to be your mum,
the one who gave you life.

(1990)

Longing

Oh my child, for you I weep,
I so long to see your face.
Into your room, I often creep,
I look around it in a daze.
It's neatness now – is ordered calm.
Your music now – is silent.
Things you loved stand all alone,
'Ghostly' – awaiting your return.
I'd love for you to come back home,
though I know that this can't be.
But I hold the honour that's mine alone,
that you came to earth – through me.

(1990)

For My Child

Care, I gave you, as well as life.
Kissed it better on arms and knees.
Cooled a burning brow with ice,
steamed the kettle, for croup and wheeze.

Many a party, for many a year.
Swimming lessons – piano too.
Many a pantomime at Christmas.
Many a worry, you never knew.

Many a grouse, many a warning,
lots of shouting, crying, sobbing,
and lots of cuddles, coming after,
and kisses until ones heart was throbbing.

Then with your prowess, came my pride,
as you grew and showed your flair,
to be yourself, as we had nurtured,
through unconditional loving care.

(1993)

Pride in Roy

If I could have you back again
If only for a day.
I could say – I've learned so much
since you went away.
I'd like to say, I'm proud of you,
and all that you achieved.
The life long fight, within your soul,
for the survival you perceived.
You won your fight, with great aplomb
more, than you could believe.

(2016)

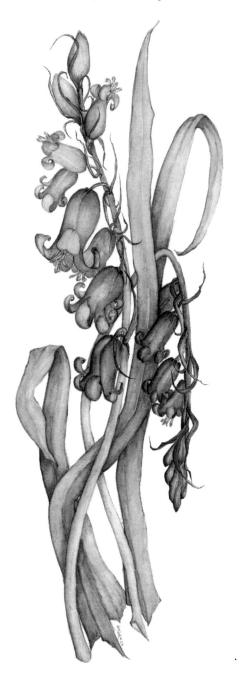

Memory

In quiet memory, tinged with love
live our own lost spirits, dear.
May peace and strength stay with you
and hold you through the fears.
Then in the quiet moments,
when your thoughts to memory turn,
the images of ones you loved
in radiance, still burn.

(1993)

Fleeting Moments

In the dusk of evening
as it ends another day.
Once again your image comes
for a while to stay.
Then for a fleeting moment
you leave your love with me.
Then I know that I am strengthened,
for another day, you see.

(2016)

Hold On in Loss

Hold on my friend, this journey's long.
This, 'being in it', with no choice,
as you cry, and yearn, inside you
no-one hears your voice.

Hold on inside you – Hold on inside.
In time the visions clear,
you'll find there's more perspective,
and you'll learn to tame the fear.

You may want help – so talk it through,
there is no weakness here.
Grief is essential, for soul and mind,
as time lapses, it's so clear.

There is no measured time span,
cherish those lost, hold on – and live.
Hold on to them, inside you,
in time, deep peace, it gives.

(2016)

For Kelvin

After his father and brother have gone so quickly.

Our family – so depleted
as those we love are gone.
As now there's only two of us
to weep – and struggle on.
For you, my son, have lost too much
so early in your life,
too young to feel this blight of loss
that brings its lonely anger, thus
inside, to contemplate, and bear.
This, is the hollow state we share.

(1990)

Later in the Mourning

In Time

Deep and quiet, remains my grief,
to break in silver shards.
When something touches memory,
sweet music or a card.

But I can hold it now within,
so only I will know.
Then if I'm in safe company,
my silver shards, I'll show.

(2017)

'My Wish for You'

Weep, oh weep for me a little,
grieve for me not a measured while.
As your life goes slowly onward,
think of me, and raise a smile.
And soon, you'll smile much more than weep,
so peace may drop its dew.
To heal the space, where I once dwelt,
when I was there – with you.
Then inside, my essence keep.
Open your soul and feel,
so I may live there every day,
and you'll always know – I'm real.

(2017)

Your Sparkle

Oh sparkle for me in the sky
when day has turned to night.
Oh show me where you are by day
in every songbirds flight.
Touch my hand, when I touch the flowers
so I may feel you're there.
All this may help my journey,
and re-imburse your care.
I need this re-assurance
to transcend the deepest sorrows,
to know your love is with me,
through all my long tomorrows.

(2017)

Feel Me

Feel me, in your inmost soul
as my heart with yours entwines.
Feel my love, protecting you,
as each day, we still combine.
Feel me in your thoughts today
don't let my memory sever.
Feel me all around your world.
Feel me in you, forever.

(1991)

My Hope for You

Beside my grave, I see you stand
and weep your silent tears.
With breaking heart in emptiness
as you think of future years.

Yet I am not there beneath the ground,
my spirits free as air.
Look around and in all you see,
know that I'll be there.

In singing birds, and in the sun,
where shadows fall – there's me.
And in bubbling rushing water
and with the stars, I'll be.

I will never leave you
I'm always in your mind,
always in your quiet thoughts
I won't be hard to find.

So weep as much as you need yourself
to release your aching heart,
and though you cannot see me,
let the healing start.

Remember now, my spirit lives
in the deeps and sky above,
then I can return, and come to you
through your unconditional love.

(1991)

Hope

In the early pearls of morning
that fall as dew on grass.
May your spirit be uplifted
as through this time you pass.

May natures love caress you
along with support from friends.
And you will know from their kind words
that caring never ends.

May your own strength uphold you
along with love sincere,
and guide you, through your sorrow
until your clouds shall clear.

(1990)

Acknowledgement

Hear the words I say to you
each and every night.
Hear the warmth of love they bring
with awareness of hindsight.

Now I know – oh so much more
about you, and your deepest scar,
and can you feel my love tonight?
It is where you are.

(2016)

Soul of My Soul,

Soul of my soul
at my innermost door.
Black is black and colour no more,
the pathways of loss,
or the shock of its hold.
Now my heart trembles as
Your hand's grown so cold.

The vibrance of your inner mind,
shall stay inside me down the years.
Its depth we shared together,
with humour, love, and tears.

Soul of my soul,
at my innermost door.
The colour is changing, a light is within,
it's time now that's needed,
with time I shall win.

(2016)

Time

How can a year have passed by,
   since your soul was called away?
I hope it found a peaceful place
   to heal, and perchance to stay.

You deserve your rest in time,
   so your suffering could cease.
You fought to live, through pain, then death
   and so have earned release.

I miss you here so deeply,
   but I now can truly say,
that if your soul has found its peace,
   I'll give thanks for that, each day.

                         (2017)

Now

I know I feel your presence,
 I feel it more and more.
The comfort in its warming
 penetrates me to my core.
The years we stood together,
 are meaning so much more.

This journey isn't easy,
 it will always be the same.
I still miss your vibrant beauty
 and your senses all aflame.
Your wit I hear inside me,
 your flippancy – with no shame.

Now I know – I can go forward.
Now I know – I'll be okay.
Now I know – that I shall make it.
As you come to me each day.
Thank you for our lifetime
 as in my heart you stay.

       (2017)